My E

by Tisha Hamilton

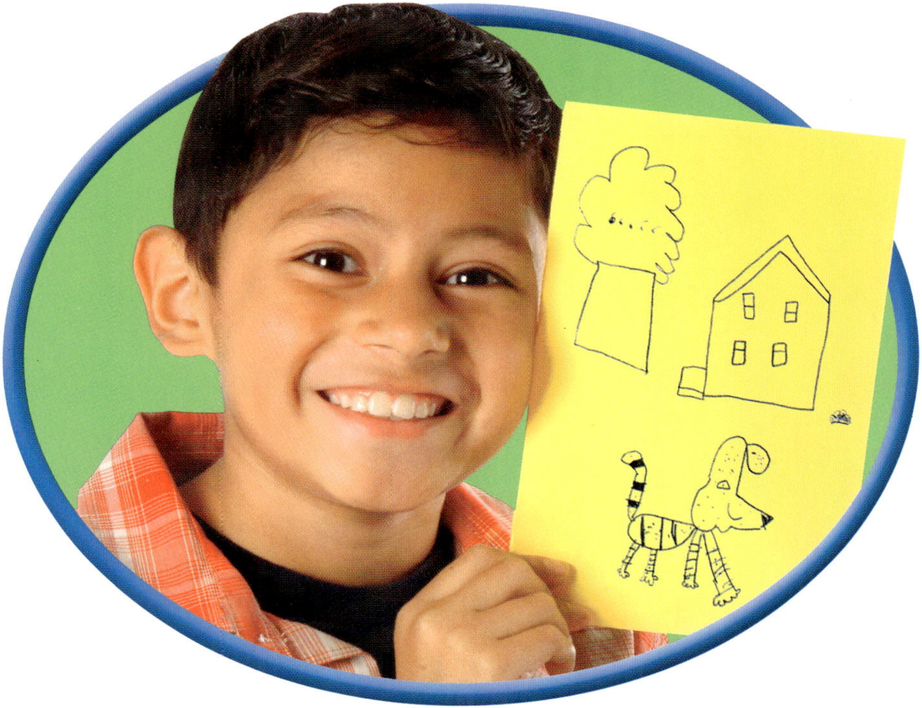

This is my school.

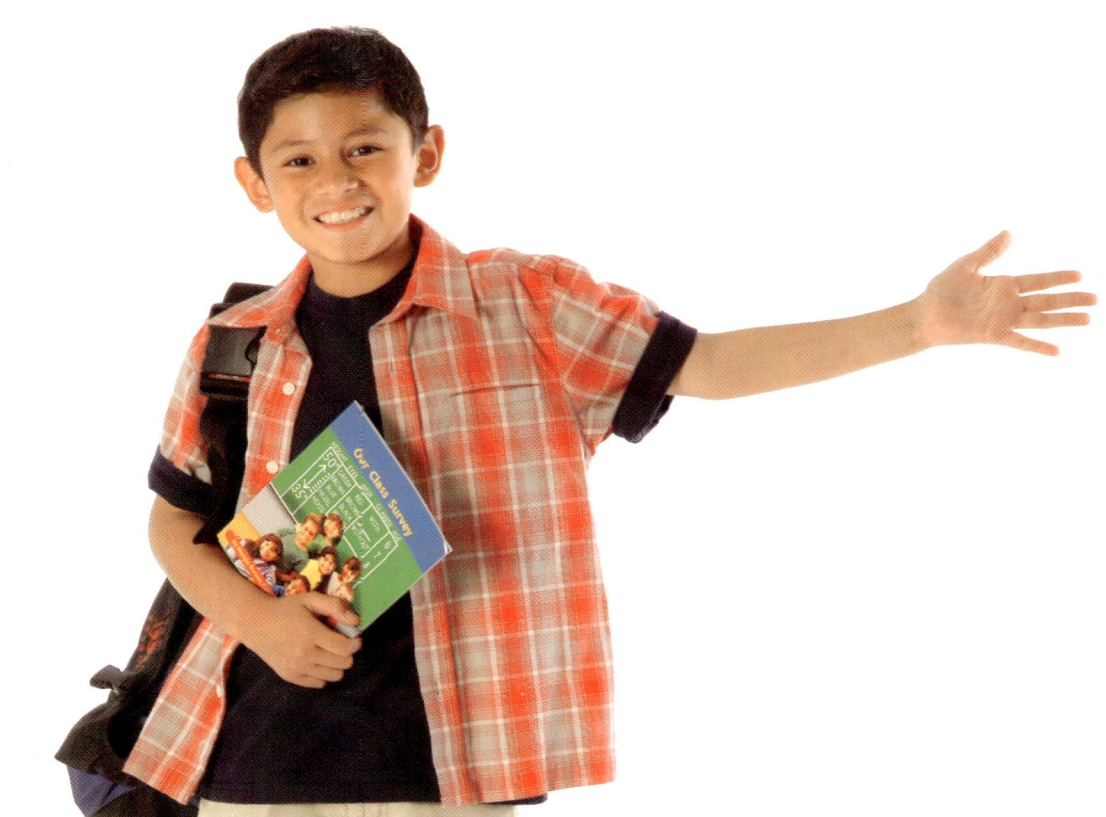

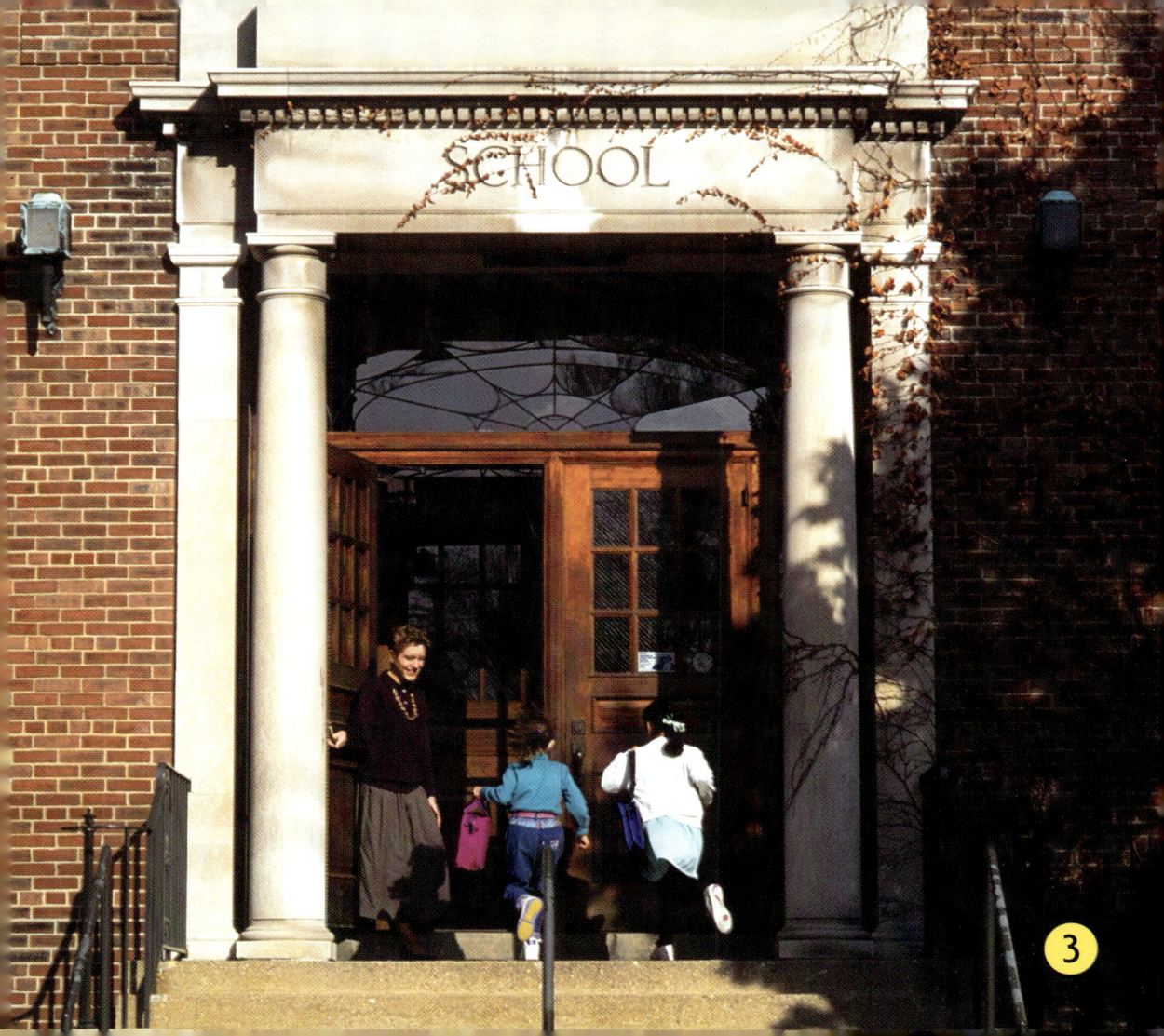

This is my class.

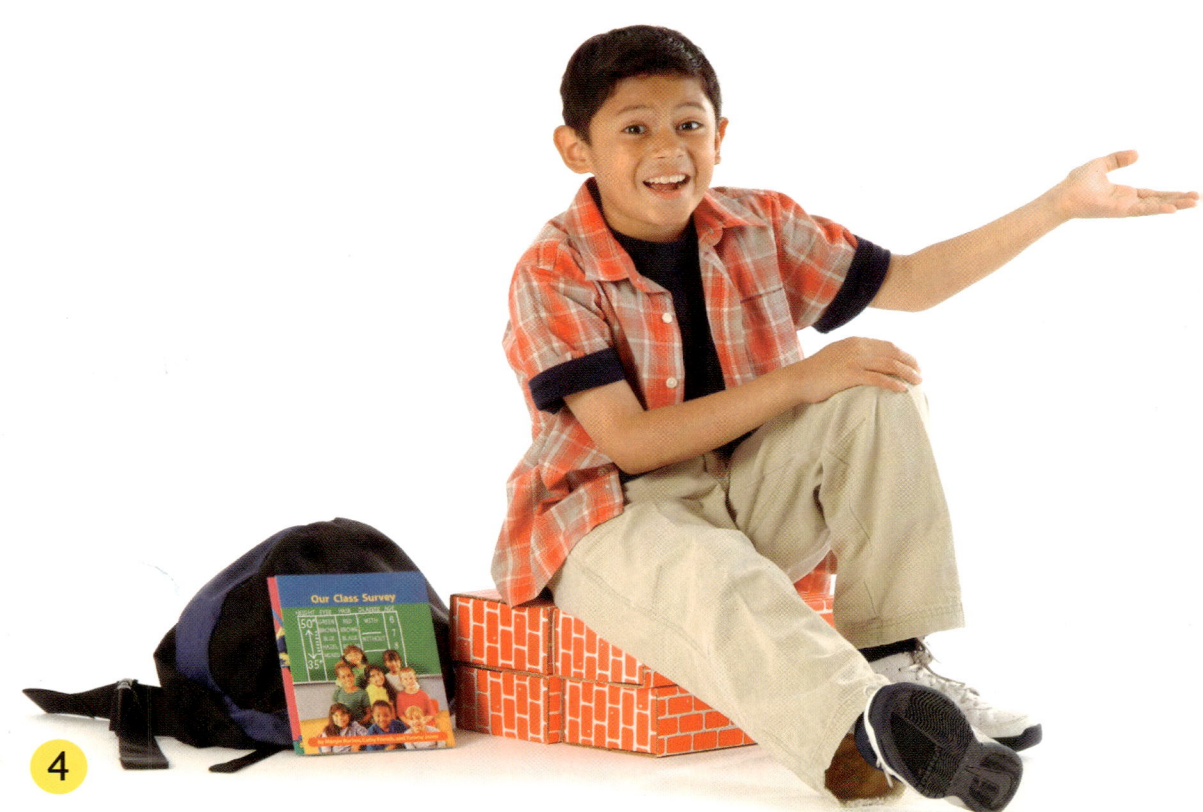

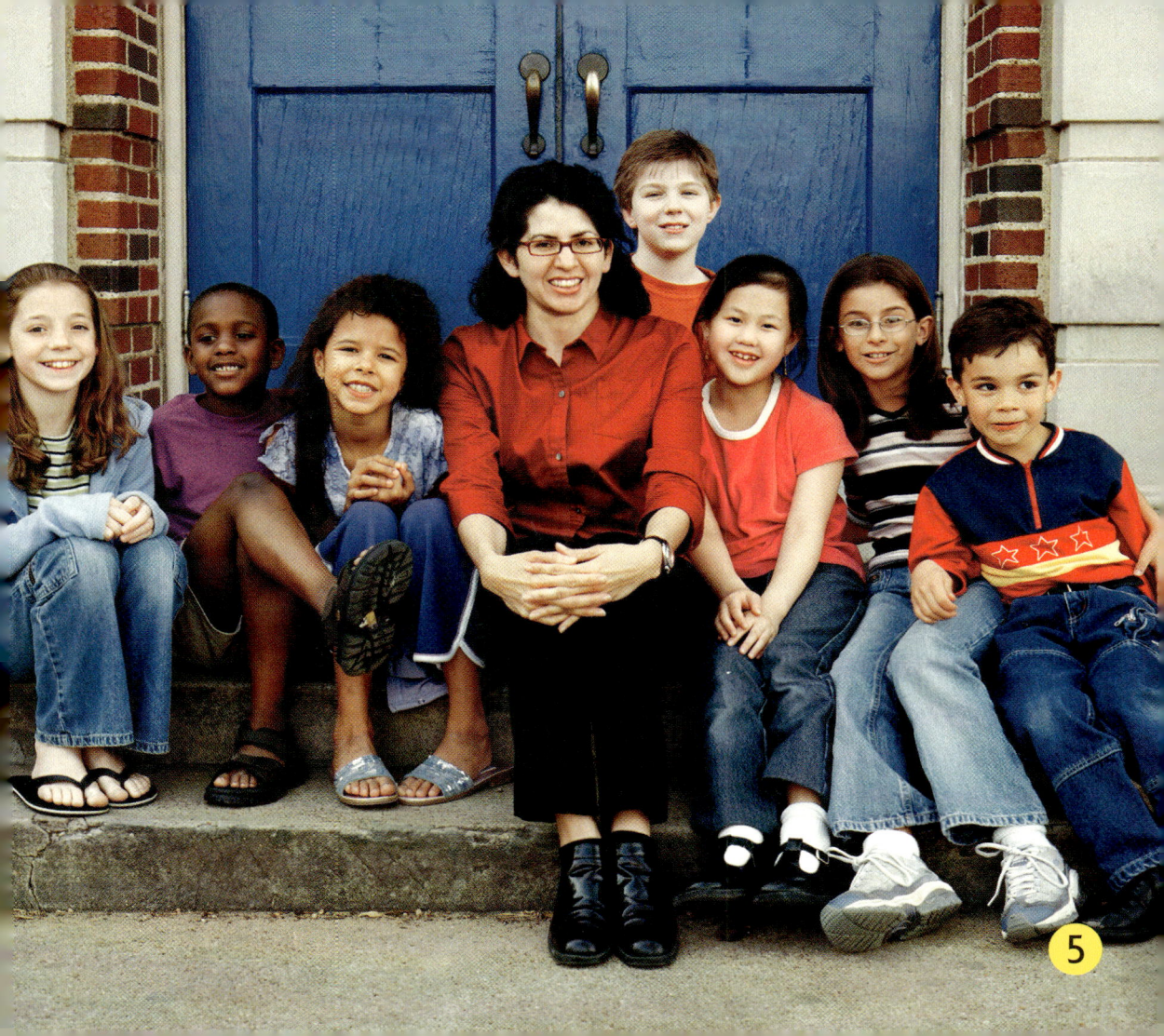

This is my paper.

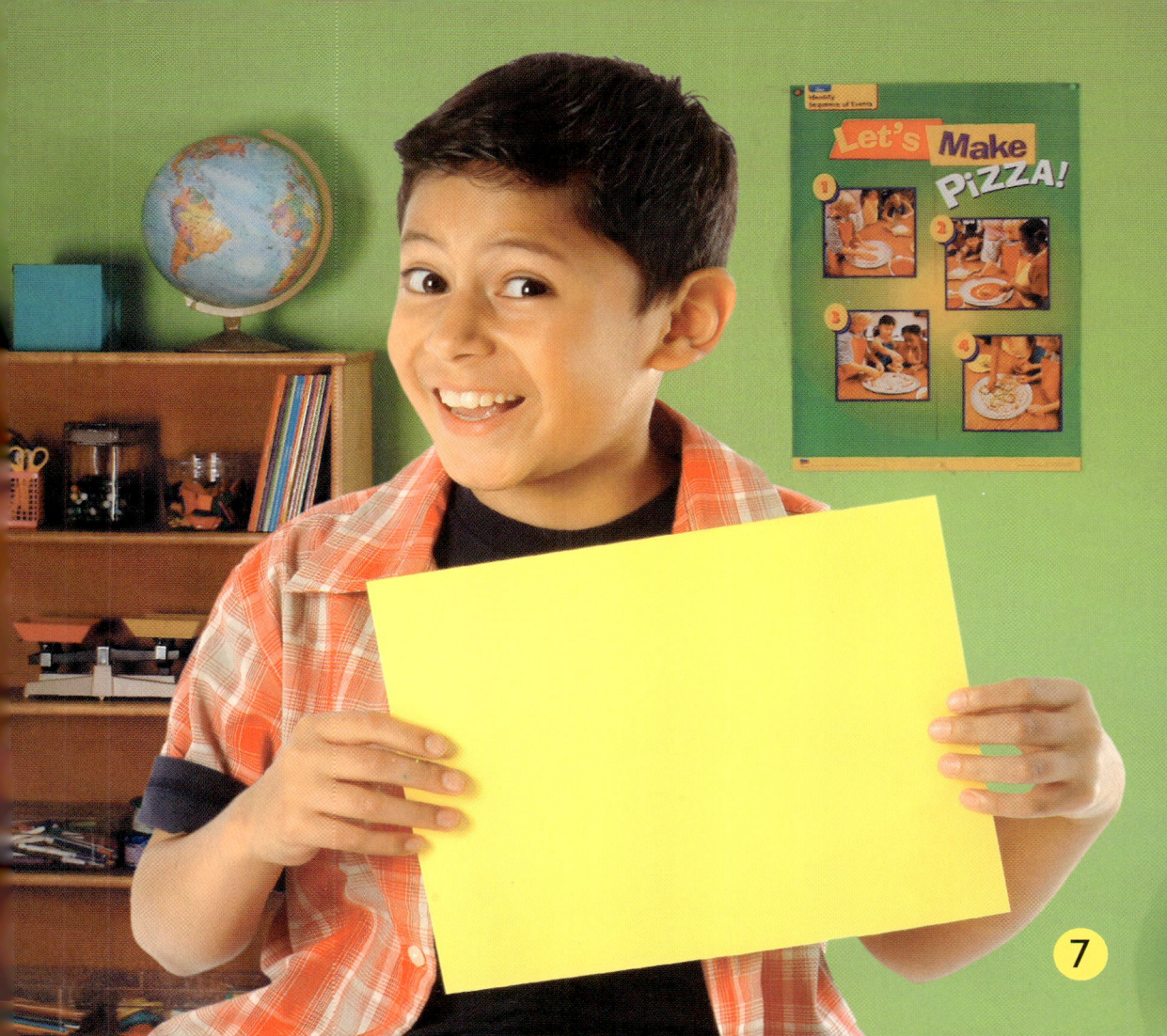

This is my pencil.

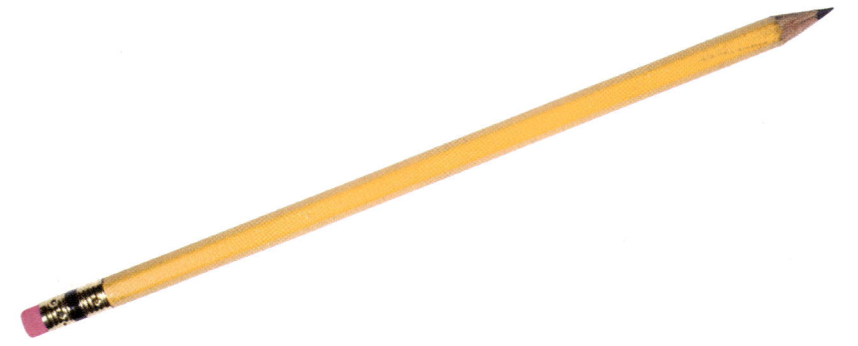

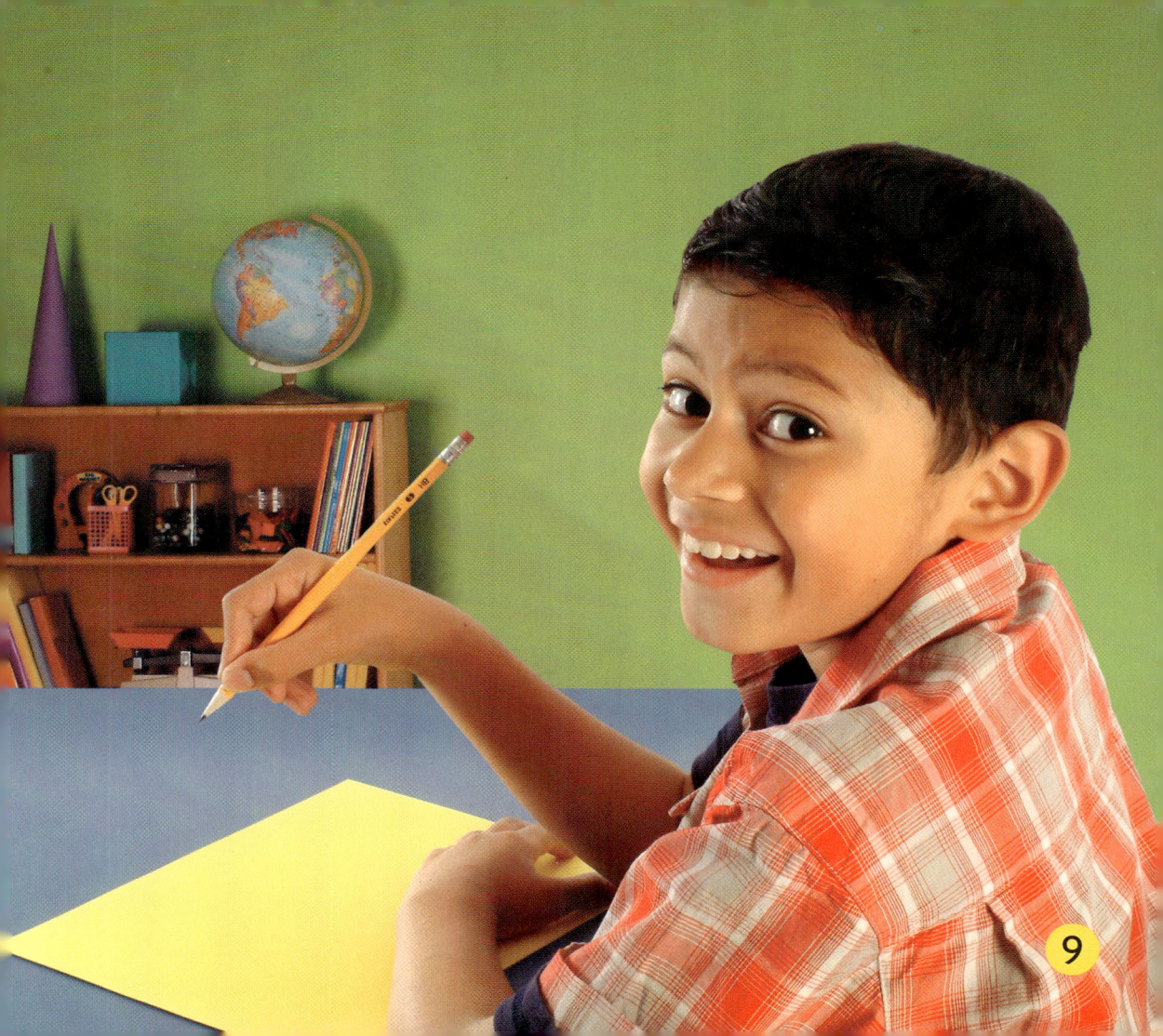

This is my house.

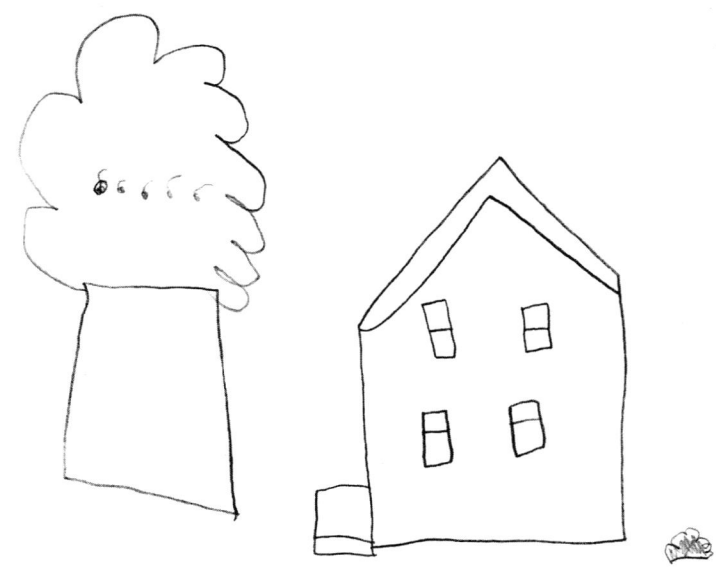

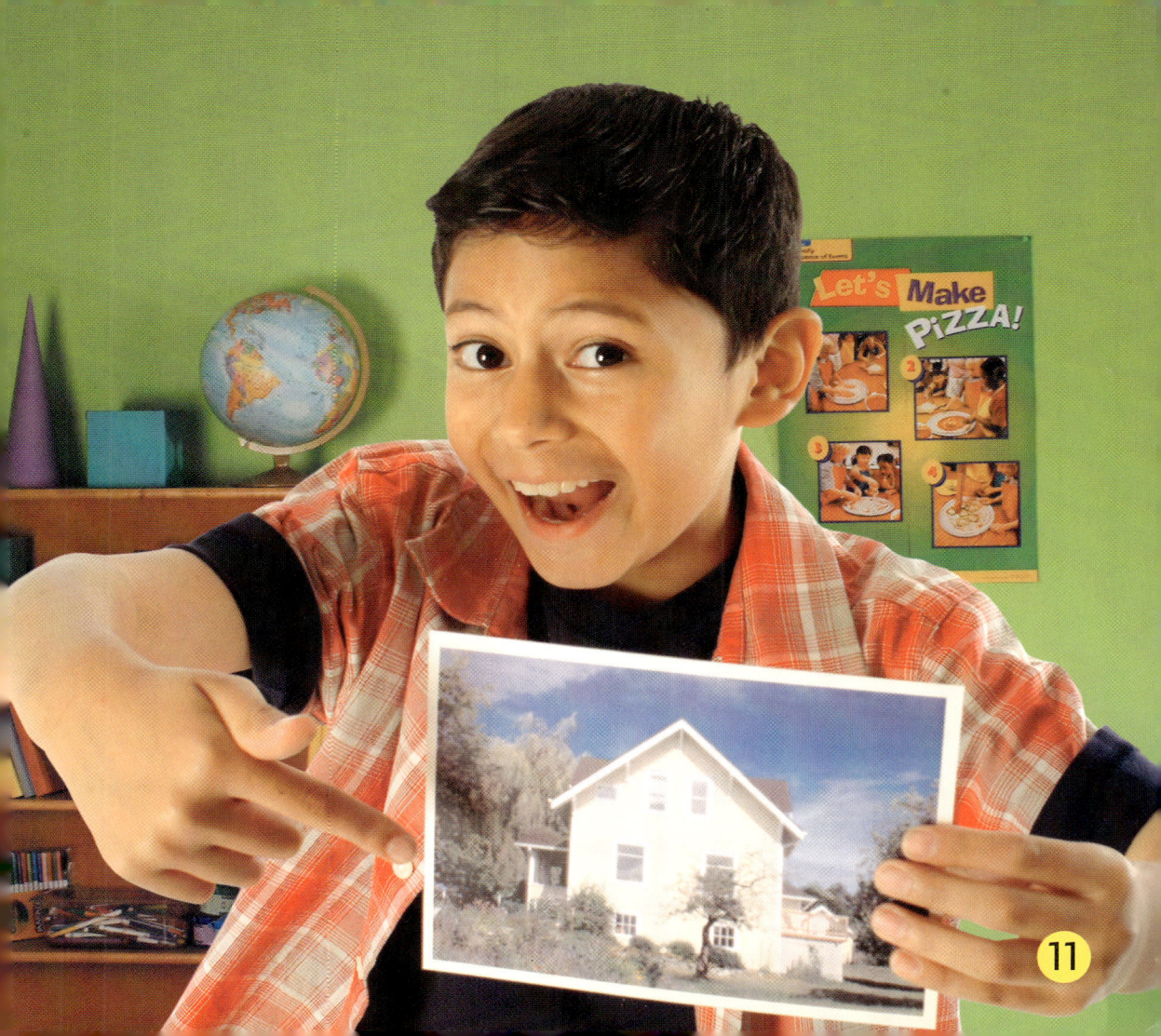

This is my dog.

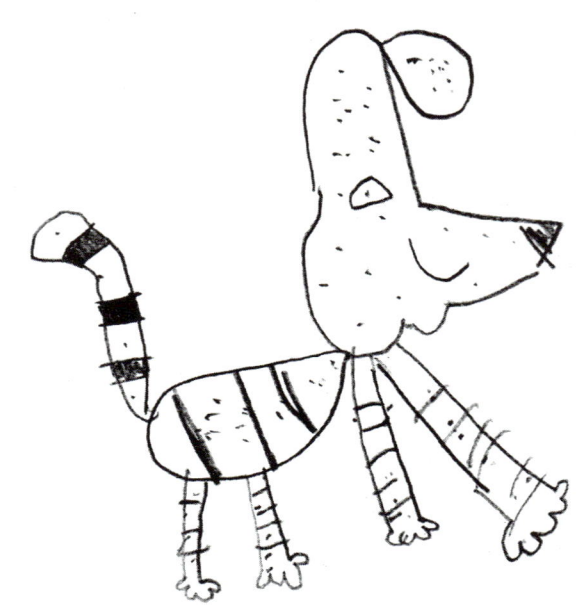

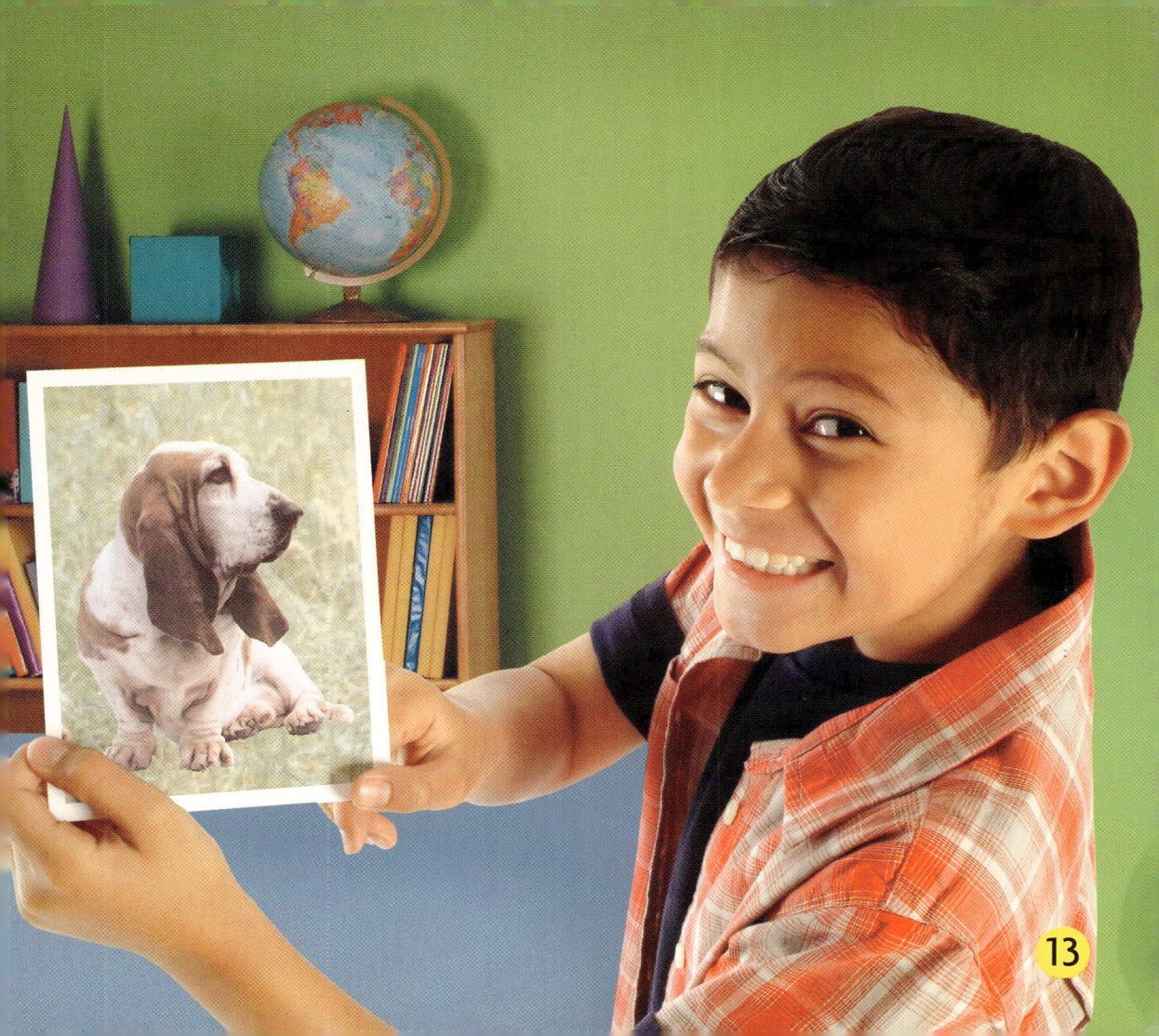

13

This is my picture.

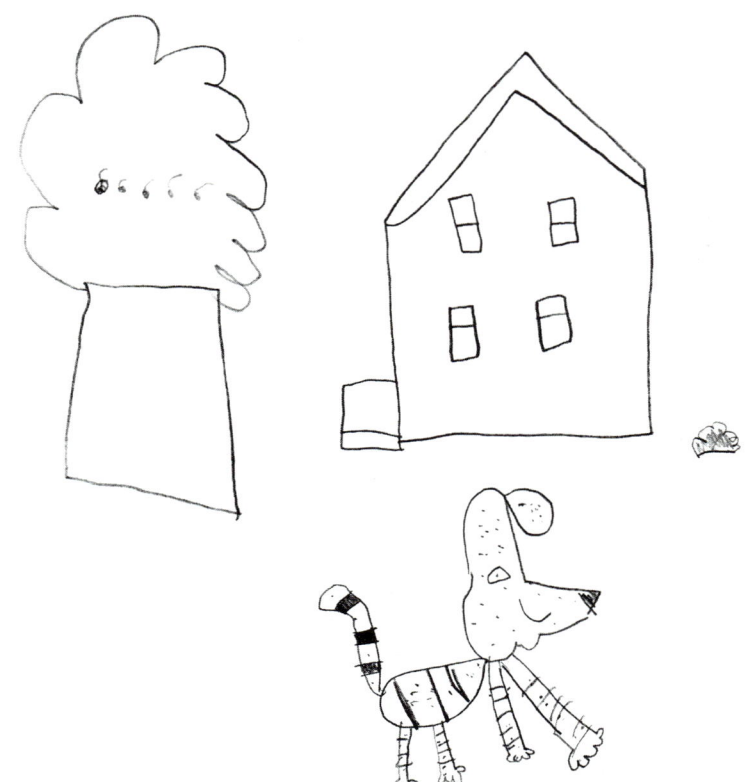

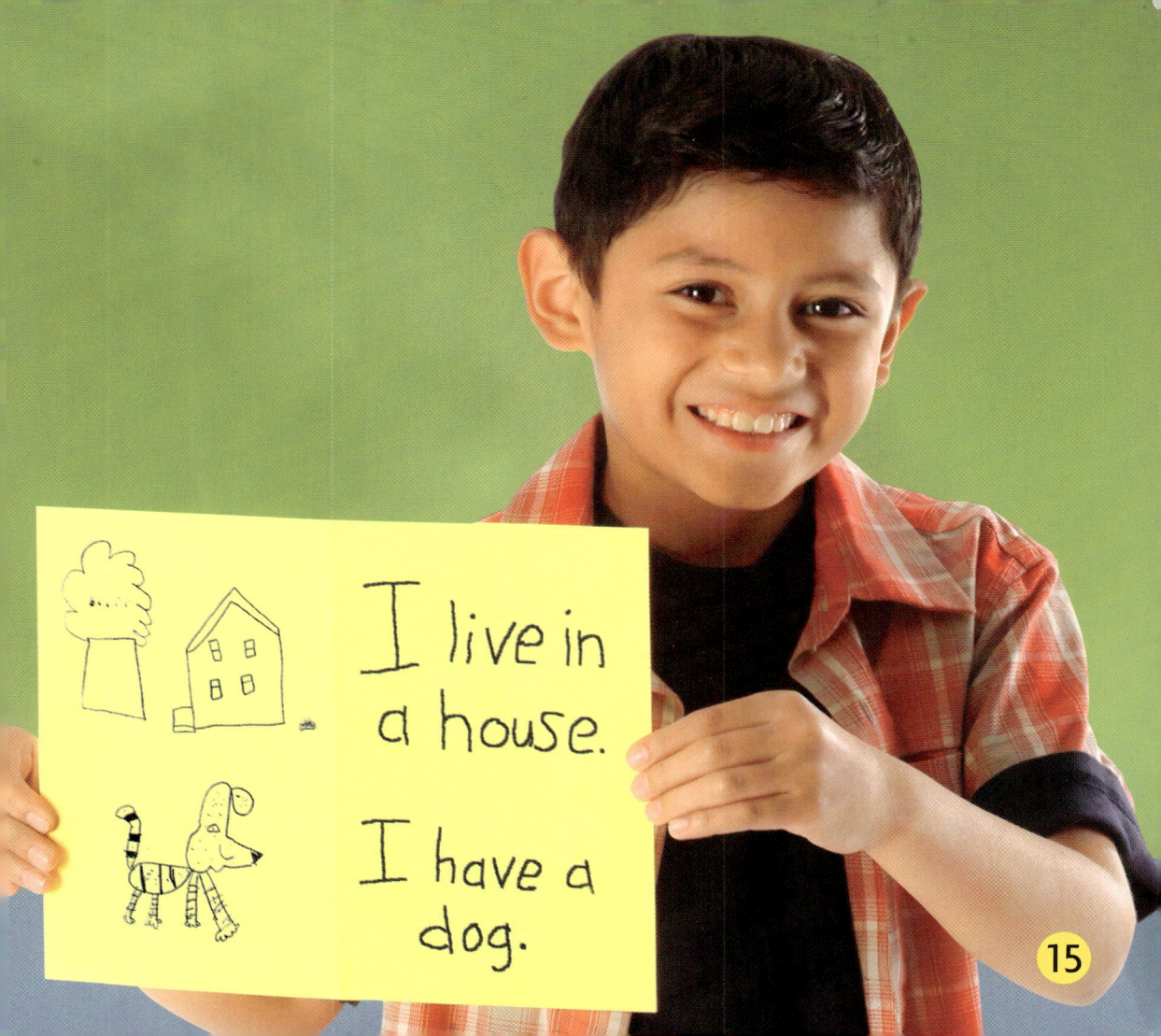

I live in a house.

I have a dog.

15

This is my book.

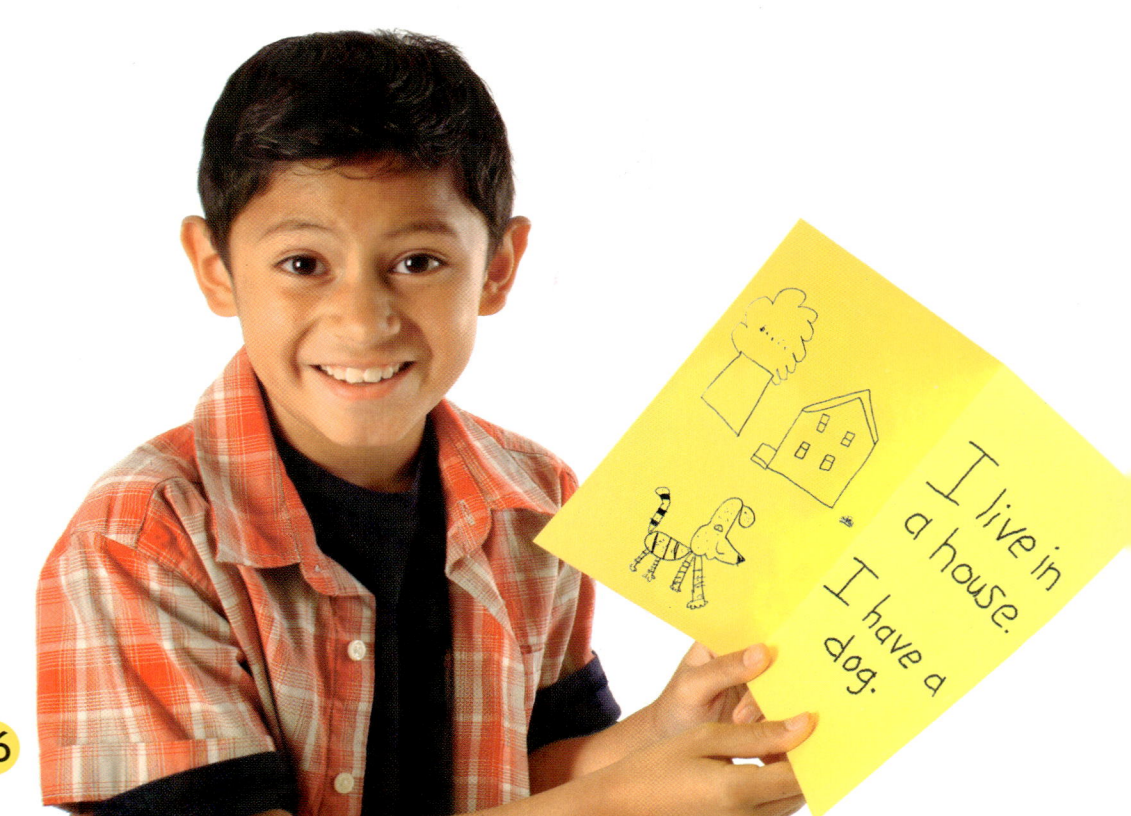